What Research Says to the Tea

Educational Games

Simulations

by Wm. Ray Heitzmann

Heitzmann, William
M
14

nea
National Education Association
Washington, D.C.

Quoted material included in this book may use the pronoun "he" to denote an abstract individual, e.g., "the student." We have not attempted to alter this material, although we currently use "she/he" in such instances.

—NEA Publishing

Copyright © 1974
National Education Association of the United States

Stock No.: 0-8106-1030-2 00

Library of Congress Cataloging in Publications Data

Heitzmann, William Ray.
    Educational games and simulations.

    (What research says to the teacher)
    Bibliography: p.
    1. Education—Simulation methods. 2. Educational games. I. Title.
LB1029.S53H44   371.3   74-16182

CONTENTS

A Recent Development? 5

   Commonly Used Classroom Games 6
   Definitions 7

Play: Its Function in Development 8

   Play in Theories of Development 8
   Play: Research Findings 9
   Play: Implications 10

Classroom Climate and Learning 10

   Psychological Climate 10
   Student-Centered Learning 11
   Group Processes 12
   Implications for Teachers 12

Diversity and Commonality 13

   Commercial Games and Simulations 13
   Teacher-Made Games and Simulations 15

Format and Procedures 16

Student Motivation 17

Cognitive Growth 18

   Factual Knowledge 18
   Intellectual Skills 19

Affective Learning 19

   Attitudinal Change 19

Summary 20

The Future 21

Selected Research References 22

General References 30

Dr. Wm. Ray Heitzmann, a member of the faculty of Villanova University, has been a teacher in the public schools of Illinois and New York. He is the author of several articles on the social studies curriculum and other related educational subjects.

The manuscript was reviewed by Dr. Don LaDue of Temple University and by Mr. John Morgan who teaches at Middletown High School, Middletown, Delaware.

A RECENT DEVELOPMENT?

The current interest in simulation and gaming is noticeable not only within schools but in society at large. In fact when one examines bookshelves (*Games People Play, The War Game, Games Christians Play, Man At Play, Man, Play and Games*), movie marquees and television programs (*The Only Game in Town, Games, The Name of the Game,* "The Dating Game," and "The Newlywed Game") could easily lead one to the conclusion that play and games have become a major preoccupation of Americans. In addition, games lining the shelves of department stores range from *Women's Lib, Blacks and Whites,* and *The Godfather* to *Jonathan Livingston Seagull* and *Watergate Scandal.*

While the present simulation and game explosion may lead one to conclude that the appearance of games is a contemporary phenomenon, in reality their origins can be traced back thousands of years. Ancient China had a war game entitled "Wei-Hai" (Encirclement) (34) and India had "Chaturanga" which is claimed to be the forerunner of chess. (60) Chess, of course, was a product of the Middle Ages and is still one of the most popular board games. Abbé Gaultier, an émigré who fled from France to England at the time of the French Revolution, invented several children's games concerned with social teaching which were widely used in England during the late eighteenth century. The art of war gaming received an impetus from the Prussians who developed it at the Kriegsacademie (War School), which was founded following the defeats administered to them by Napoleon. (18) During this century the U.S. military copied the Prussian example with success. After World War II American business, impressed by the military use of simulated training techniques, developed several games for management training. Of course Parker Brothers' *Monopoly*, a product of the 1930's, exists as the most popular board game.

It was during the 1960's that the potential learning value of simulations and games became recognized by teachers of elementary and secondary school students. Of course teachers have long appreciated the learning value of games: Alcuin used academic puzzles in teaching students at Charlemagne's Court School and the "Spelling Bee", a favorite during the last century is still with us today.

Commonly Used Classroom Games

Games have for many years been used for drill and review. In using them teachers found that students were not only learning content but were developing the ability to work together. In addition, students were found to be motivated by the game format, so it was natural for teachers to begin to use games along with other instructional techniques.

Some classroom games in use by teachers are "Who Am I?", "College Bowl", and various card and sports games. In "Who Am I?" the teacher divides the class into teams which then review characteristics of historical figures, chemicals, plants, literary characters, artists, musicians, or authors (depending on the course), and the class at the same time constructs questions to be used in the game. The game finds each team in turn trying to guess the answer based upon the characteristics given by a member of the other team. Points are awarded upon the success of the opposing team in correctly guessing the answer to "Who Am I?"

"College Bowl" closely parallels the popular television program. Usually the class prepares questions beforehand which are then drawn out of a box and asked of the appropriate team members. Many times teachers modify the game to enable more students to participate, for example, by involving the audience, using several teams, or frequently rotating the teams.

Card games likewise take many forms. Typical is "Authors" in which the players proceed as in traditional card games, only in this game a player makes a "pair" by matching the author and the author's work. Variations of the game can be used in other subject areas—matching an historical figure or a scientist with his achievement. Commercially prepared card games also include "Euro Card," designed to develop a student's knowledge of Europe through map orientation and "AL PHA BET" which is useful for spelling and vocabulary improvement.

Presently the number of learning games and simulations is expanding greatly. Zuckerman and Horn in their recent work, *The Guide to Simulations/Games* (1973), list over 600 entries, a fifty percent increase over their previous volume published two years earlier. (72) Obviously the Zuckerman-Horn book does not include most of the teacher-made simulations and games which are also developing at a rapid rate. The growth of this aspect of teaching strategy can be appreciated when one considers that virtually no teacher-made games existed in the early sixties. This technique with its ability to motivate, actively involve students in learning, encourage group cooperation, stimulate enthusiasm for learning, and inject realism into the classroom situation has captured the imagination of teacher and student alike and established itself as an important teaching methodology.

Definitions

Learning games designed for use in classrooms have been given various titles and definitions. While for purposes of this paper the terms *game* and *simulation* will be used interchangeably, the following are some generally accepted technical definitions by game designers, games researchers, and teachers:

Game (Gaming)

A game is essentially a simplified slice of reality. Its structure reflects a real world process that the designer wishes to teach or investigate: the game serves as a vehicle for testing that process or for learning more about its working. . . . (5)

Alice Kaplan Gordon

Games are activities with goals and rules. (49)

Samuel A. Livingston
Clarice Stasz Stoll

(A game is a) contest (play) among adversaries (players) operating unders constraint (rules) for an objective (winning, victory or payoff). (1)

Clark C. Abt

7

Simulation

A simulation is a replica of a real world situation worth learning. An educational simulation permits a person to become a working member of the system, to set goals, to develop policies, analyze information. (43)

Ron Klietsch

Essentially, simulation is a means of allowing the student to live vicariously. Furthermore, the simulation has the desirable quality of enabling the teacher to manipulate various courses of action and their consequences without the students suffering physically for wrong choices. (10)

Samuel Brodbelt

Simulation is a model of a situation (social, mathematical or physical) with reality simplified; it permits the operation upon a specifically devised problem in a time sequence method. (13)

June R. Chapin

PLAY: ITS FUNCTION IN DEVELOPMENT

Closely related to the use of learning games and simulations is the psychological and physiological concept of play. Almy, a psychologist who has devoted much of her efforts to the study and research of play, states her feeling as to the value and significance of play:

. . . .Play provides the opportunity not only to savour whatever pleasurable aspects the experience had and in various ways to work out compensations for its hurts but also to understand it. . . .
One might well conclude that it provides a setting for the exercise of certain abilities involved in thinking and reasoning. It is as though the child, freed from the handicaps eventually to be imposed by logic and some of the realities of space and time could try out incipient intellectual power. (4)

Play in Theories of Development

Many psychologists, educators and educational theorists have long seen fit to comment on play and its relationship to growth and development. Plato, Comenius, Pestalozzi and Froebel all took into account the interest of children in play when formulating their educational systems. While Herbert

8

Spencer saw play as a result of "surplus energy" and G. Stanley Hall explained it in terms of recapitulation (the child repeats in play the interests and occupations of prehistoric and primitive man), more recently the work of Freud and Piaget has established play as more than "frivolous activity." (57) Freud and Piaget have theorized that play is important to one's emotional and intellectual development. Freud saw play as the reenactment of unpleasant events and suggested "play therapy" as a technique to aid disturbed children. Most recently Piaget has postulated that play is important for cognitive development.

Piaget's theory of play is tightly bound to his explanation of the growth of intelligence. Assimilation and accomodation are two processes he believes to be fundamental to development. (He views assimilation as analogous to the child changing when confronted by a situation in the environment, for example, moving to avoid an obstacle.) Piaget sees these two complementary processes in terms of cognitive development thus: Assimilation is the process which takes in the information the child receives, changes it, and makes it become part of the child's knowledge. Accommodation means the adjustment of the organism to assimilate the information. Cognitive growth takes place when these two processes are in equilibrium. For Piaget, cognitive development proceeds through a sequence of relative discontinuous stages; underlying this progression is the interaction of these two processes. (62)

Play enters the theory as pure assimilation, providing different value during the various stages of development. Consequently, play is necessary for the child's intellectual growth.

The warning of the eminent psychologist Bruno Bettelheim seems significant in this regard.

> If we gave children the opportunity to play, maybe some of them would not be driven to compensate for time lost by playing 'revolution' or 'cops and robbers' in their twenties. (8)

Play: Research Findings

There seems to be support among educators and developmental psychologists for the position that play contributes to one's intellectual growth, imagination, and creativity. (69, 21)

In one study dealing with play, it was found that there was a positive correlation between divergent thinking and playfulness. (46) In the same vein Charlotte Buhler found that "children deprived of creative play. . . .grow up deficient in imagination and inhibited in experience." (18)

In a different context group play therapy sessions can contribute to the better emotional stability of group members. (5)

Play: Implications

Obviously classroom teachers wish to contribute to the intellectual development and growth of their students. A form of play, learning games and educational simulations can serve as useful vehicles in this regard enabling, teachers to aid their students to achieve these objectives in a useful, constructive way.

CLASSROOM CLIMATE AND LEARNING

Psychological Climate

During the 1930's Kurt Lewin, a psychologist, emphasized the importance of the "psychological environment" in relation to human development. (44) He and later his students related to this concept such variables as "democratic atmosphere," "frustration" and "regression" as they contributed to the environment. Research built upon these ideas in educational settings found the classroom climate to be important in terms of student achievement. (20)

Recently there has been a strong emphasis upon the importance of the affect of the classroom climate. Stirling M. McMurrin defines the affective function of teaching as follows:

> The affective function of instruction pertains to the practical life—to the emotions, the passions, the dispositions, the motives, the moral and esthetic sensibilities, the capacity for feeling, concern, attachment or detachment, sympathy, empathy, and appreciation. (53)

Every teacher naturally wishes to create a classroom atmosphere in which students finish a course with a better feeling toward the subject than when they began the course. Robert Mager has provided some suggestions for teachers who ask how they can have a positive classroom climate.

> By making sure there are as few aversive conditions as possible while the student is in the presence of the subject we are teaching him. By making sure that the student's contact with the subject is followed by positive, rather than aversive, consequences. By modeling the very kind of behavior we would like to see exhibited by our students. (54)

Essentially Mager wishes teachers to eliminate those elements which will lead to negative feelings about school and the subject, such as frustration, humiliation, embarrassment, fear, anxiety, pain, and boredom.

Certain instructional strategies lend themselves to improving the positive affect of the classroom's climate. Surely educational games and simulations must rank high on this list.

Student-Centered Learning

In recent years there has been a growing trend toward student-centered learning based upon the beliefs that this will lead to greater student interest and increased learning. This seems to be supported by research findings. Group brainstorming prior to a task was found to have positive results in that students were more productive and creative after having the opportunity to brainstorm. (70, 47)

An important finding in one research study reached the following results:

> The teacher-centered behavior of directing, demanding, and using private criteria in deprecating a student leads to hostility to the self or teacher and aggressiveness, or sometimes withdrawal, apathy, and even emotional disintegration.

> The learner-centered behavior of accepting the student, being evaluative or critical only by public criteria, and being usually supportive elicited problem-orientation, decreased personal anxiety, and led to emotionally readjusting and integrative behavior. (29)

Additional studies have corroborated the above conclusions. (68)

Group Processes

As learning games and educational simulations characteristically take place in group settings of various sizes, it is important to be aware of the research literature on leadership. For many years a study on leadership by Kurt Lewin and his associates, which identified the democratic style as the most effective, stood as the guide for classroom management. (45) Additional studies supported this finding: Selvin found that authoritarian and *laissez-faire* leadership atmospheres resulted in less desirable behaviors among the groups studied than did democratic leadership. (66) Coach and French concluded that "total participation" resulted in significant improvement in productivity among workers involved in that participation. (15) While generally the democratic style is believed to be the most successful, the work of Flanders gives teachers important advice when he concludes that "flexibility"—the ability to adopt a wide range of roles—is consistent with good teaching and resulting high student achievement. (30) That is, there are certain times and conditions that call for the teacher to adopt an authoritarian, a democratic, or a *laissez-faire* role.

Another area of leader behavior related to group processes is what has been called the "human relations" dimension—"structure" and "consideration." In several studies relating these two concepts it has been found that the most desirable relationship occurs when a leader is high in consideration and high in structure. (See opposite) In addition it was also concluded that consideration is the more critical of the two attributes, a finding which meshes with some of the research mentioned earlier in this report.

Implications for Teachers

Educational games and simulations exist as possibilities for presenting a student-centered environment in a structured way. These teaching strategies provide an opportunity for the classroom teacher to incorporate into her or his repertoire of methodologies a flexible, democratic, learner-centered technique that will contribute to students' affective and cognitive growth.

X UNDESIRABLE

X DESIRABLE

CONSIDERATION

X UNDESIRABLE

STRUCTURE

Adapted from
Fleishman, Harris (31)

When one considers that research has clearly demonstrated that most classes are non-student centered (67, 61) the learning value of this technique is even more significant, because games and simulations exist as potentially dynamic devices for focusing more consistently on the student.

DIVERSITY AND COMMONALITY

The current expansion of learning games and educational simulations has proceeded in many directions, and consequently, there has been no standardization. Twelker analyzes the situation thus:

> Games vary enormously. They are designed for different target populations, for different levels of sophistication, for different subject matter, for various sizes of teams and numbers and players, and so on. (71)

While it is true that diversity dominates the field, there does exist some commonality of characteristics such as the following:

1. A conflict of interest is represented to involve the student actively.
2. The student assumes an active role in contrast with traditional learning experiences found in a school.
3. The student has some alternatives from which to choose and typically some control over events.
4. Immediate feedback is frequently part of the process and the consequences of decisions are relayed quickly to the students. (55)

Commercial Games and Simulations

The popularity of these education methodologies has been estimated to constitute a sales market well in excess of $100,000,000. (71) In fact the expansion of the market has given rise to several new companies which deal solely in this field. Commercial games have taken many forms, of which the following are representative examples. "Man: A Course of Study,"* a program used in the middle grades, contains three games as part of the course. In a similar fashion Science Research Associates developed six American History simulations in connection with their *Promise of America* textbook. Likewise, many of the curriculum projects also integrate into their units games such as *Farming* which is part of the High School Geography Project. Some simulations produced by major textbook publishers include *Get Set*, eight reading readiness games available from Houghton Mifflin, *Dangerous Parallel*, a sophisticated social science simulation available from Scott Foresman, and SRA's *Inter-Nation Simulation.*

---

*It is unfortunate that the title should make this course appear to exclude women.

However, many games are marketed by smaller organizations such as: *Equations*, by Maret Company, *Crisis* by Simile II, *Pollution* by Wellesley Schools Curriculum Center. Additional games are available from such diverse sources as the National Training Labs, the National Education Association (the *Governance* game) selected issues of educational journals, instructional journals such as *Scholastic Search*, and most issues of the *Simulation-Gaming-News*.

Teacher-Made Games and Simulations

Frequently teachers find that, despite the quality of commercially available instructional materials, they have difficulty integrating them into their units and lessons. Consequently many teachers have designed their own games commensurate with the abilities and interests of their students and their course content and objectives. Clark Abt, professional game designer has formulated ten steps to follow in designing a game:

1. Define overall *objectives* (teaching, analysis, design, tests, exploration, etc.).
2. Determine *scope* (duration, geographic area, issues).
3. Identify key *actors* (individual groups or organizations making the critical decisions).
4. Determine *actors' objectives* (power, wealth, influence, etc., in specific contexts).
5. Determine *actors' resources* (physical, social, economic, political, information).
6. Determine the *interaction sequence among the actors* (flow of resources and information to and from each actor).
7. Determine the *decisions rules* or criteria on the basis of which actors decide what resources and information to transmit or receive or what actions to take.
8. Identify *external constraints* on actions of the actors (such as no violence being permitted in a competition among Quakers).
9. Formulate *scoring rules* or *win criteria* on the basis of the degree to which actors or teams of actors achieve their objectives with efficient utilization of resources.
10. Choose form of presentation and manipulation (board game, role play, paper/pencil exercise, computer simulation), and formulate *sequence of operations*. (2)

Additional suggestions and ideas concerning designing learning games and educational simulations may be obtained from the items listed under General References at the end of this report.

FORMAT AND PROCEDURES

Educational games and simulations fall into four basic patterns—paper and pencil, role playing, board games, and combinations of the first three. *Monopoly* is the classic board game which also rests upon the role playing of the participants; it is representative in that it combines the basic patterns into an effective game.

Procedures

Inbar, following a research study, has emphasized the importance of the person acting as the game facilitator, stressing that this person affects the success of the game more than expected. (39) Consequently, the teacher should be intimately familiar with the game to maximize student learning. One study concluded that the students' acceptance of the game was positively related to their comprehension of the teacher's reasons for using the simulation. (23) Almost all simulations involve group processes—dividing the class into groups which "play" against one another. In this regard McKinney and Dill "recommend against any method of grouping that puts the weaker members of the class together on teams." (52) Other studies have found the use of team competition to be valuable in increasing students' achievement. (25, 24) A couple of studies have concentrated upon the effect of the number of plays of a game upon student learning. The general conclusion reached has been that repetition of number of plays beyond two does not appreciate significantly student learning. (42, 22)

The discussion follow-up to instructional media has long been regarded as important to student learning. However, the research on the post simulation discussion is ambivalent. While some researchers have found that it has no effect on the improvement of learning, many teachers and game designers feel this is indispensable to gaming-simulation. It is important to note that some studies found post game discussion important to learning. One researcher concluded that participants in a simulation with discussion "will express more satisfaction with learning" than subjects who did not experience discussion. (11) Another found increased learning promoted "by reflection on the game experiences" (32), while still another had similar results. (41)

In terms of procedures for teachers facilitating simulations, the following "ten commandments" were formulated by Myron R. Chartier.

1. Thou shalt not correct the minor mistakes of players.
2. Thou shalt not offer a better strategy that a player does not perceive.
3. Thou shalt not review in minute detail the purposes, rules, and materials of the simulation game.
4. Thou shalt not correct any elaboration or alteration of the rules of the game by participants.
5. Thou shalt not keep perfect order. Gaming is fun and noisy.
6. Thou shalt not stymie any points that seem to be irrelevant to the discussion. They often are relevant, or at worst, only brief digressions.
7. Thou shalt not constrain the moderate physical movements a game may require.
8. Thou shalt not answer participants' questions about the game with 'That's not in the rules!' It is impossible for the designers of a simulation game to account for all events and questions that might arise in the course of playing.
9. Thou shalt admit thy lack of knowledge about a point of the game's operation under study.
10. Thou shalt consider a simulation game as serious a form of education as less enjoyable forms. (12)

STUDENT MOTIVATION

One of the most consistent and strongest claims made for using educational games has been their motivational value. No doubt this has strongly (if not solely) contributed to the popularity of the medium. That high student interest is associated with participation in simulations can easily be documented. Conclusions such as "experimentation indicates that they are powerful motivators" (9), have been reached by many researchers with diverse games in several settings. (17, 33, 14) Of interest is one study in which school absences decreased seventeen percent at a time when games were being used. (16)

Perhaps more important with regard to motivation is the fact that students who have been classified as "underachievers," "disadvantaged" (culturally different) and "inner city" have shown strong interest in educational games and have profited from them in terms of learning. (27, 16, 50)

Students' enjoyment of simulations seems to be related to their need for active, rather than passive, involvement. Students can have input in the outcome of the event. Simulations permit students to utilize their natural tendencies—walking, talking, and they often require group involvement and healthy competition. Finally they offer a respite from the more routine classroom procedures.

COGNITIVE GROWTH

While it is important that student interests be respected in planning for instruction, the function of instruction is cognitive and affective change.

Factual Knowledge

Several studies have concluded that students taught through educational games and simulations learn more content than do students taught in a conventional manner. While a few studies found no difference the majority reached conclusions typified by the following: Baker using a pre-Civil War simulation found "simulation classes were superior" in terms of content. (7) A game designed to promote children's language development, *Giant Steps*, was found to result in a "marked increase" in learning. (26) Cohen came to a somewhat similar conclusion with *Consumer*, a game involving players in the economics of installment buying, stating the game "appears able to teach students important concepts" because the students involved in a study acquired "a greater knowledge of terms." (16) Obviously these are findings welcomed by both teachers and administrators. However, the results of the performance of students in terms of intellectual skills is of special importance.

Intellectual Skills

While the number of studies in this area is severely limited, some of the initial work shows promise. *Wff 'N Proof*, a game involving mathematical logic, was found to increase significantly the problem-solving skills. (3) With a different simulated environment in vocational education Finch and O'Reilly found similar results, that is the improvement of problem-solving skills. (28) In the same vein, Ryan found that a simulation involving problem-solving tasks could "develop students' ability to apply (transfer) knowledge of concepts and principles." (64)

Additional studies in the area of intellectual skills have concluded that simulational games can be effective in the learning of strategies (65) and useful as "a pedagogical device for gaining insight into the process of planning." (51)

The more efficient and improved acquisition of cognitive knowledge as a result of participation in a simulation holds promise as a major advancement in the teaching-learning process.

AFFECTIVE LEARNING

While many educators are concerned with the effect that simulations have upon cognitive learning, they believe the real payoff will be in the affective domain, theorizing that active involvement learning will have a greater opportunity to facilitate attitudinal change.

With the present emphasis in curriculum development on teaching of values, values clarification, and values analysis, the effect of simulations in this area is of particular interest.

Attitudinal Change

The majority of research studies reveal that involvement in learning games and simulations can indeed change the attitude of participants. DeKock reported that following *Sunshine*, an educational simulation dealing with racial attitudes, "Their (students') attitudes are affected." (19) In a different study with the same game, Newman obtained similar results. (58) In one study with business students the simulation involved resulted in changing beliefs. (63) Another investigation involving teachers concluded that following the simulation participants were "more accepting" toward the integration of exceptional children into the regular classroom. (60) Additional studies have reached similar conclusions regarding simulations and attitudinal change. The situation is best summarized by Anderson following a study involving the *Consumer* game, "The results suggest that simulation games are better able to produce behavioral changes than conventional classroom techniques." (6) A note of caution should be made. Livingston found on a delayed post-test no significant attitudinal differences between students who played *Ghetto* and those who did not (an immediate post-test revealed changes in opinion). (48) The significance of this rests in the fact that under certain conditions with certain games there may be no permanency of attitudinal change. Despite this, the future of simulations and games in this domain does look very promising. (37)

In fact, the failure of educators to find a consistently valid instructional technique to contribute to changing attitudes has led many social psychologists to experiment with group simulations.

The problems involved in this area are the difficulties in measuring attitudes, as well as methodological pitfalls involved in the research.

SUMMARY

The generalizations suggested to teachers by research are many:

1. The interest in and expansion of simulations and games is extensive. Teachers can take advantage of interest by planning their instruction accordingly.

2. Play is important if not vital to proper social, emotional, and intellectual development. Simulations can provide opportunities for students to "play" in structured yet open ways.

3. The psychological atmosphere of the classroom is important to successful instruction. Educational games provide an opportunity for learner-centered instruction in a flexible leadership style for the teacher.

4. Many commercial simulations exist in all subject areas. In addition teachers can design their own educational games to fit their students' special situations.

5. Regardless of the type of simulations used, teachers must be knowledgeable about the game and be aware of procedures to follow and avoid to maximize learning.

6. Students are highly motivated by educational simulations and enjoy playing them.

7. Simulations have been shown to be able to teach facts and other intellectual skills as well as alter the attitudes and opinions of participants.

8. Additional investigations are needed to reach more clear conclusions on the learning value of simulations. With additional studies most educators believe that learning games will have value with students in most courses and in most situations.

THE FUTURE

So often in education instructional fads seem to grab the attention of teachers for short periods of time then disappear as quickly as they arrived. While several authors have pointed out the need for future studies with better research methodologies (35, 38), simulations promise much for both teacher and student. If critics of education are correct in their analysis that the curriculum becomes more abstract, more coldly academic, and more irrelevant as students proceed through school (40), then learning games and simulations hold out the promise to change this situation.

SELECTED RESEARCH REFERENCES

1. Abt Associates Inc. *Game Learning and Disadvantaged Groups.* Cambridge, Mass.: Abt. 1965.

2. Abt, Clark C. Abt Associates Inc. 1967.

3. Allen, Layman E., Robert W. Allen, and James C. Miller. "Programmed Games and the Learning of Problem-Solving Skills: The Wff 'N Proof Example." *The Journal of Educational Research.* 60: 22-25. September 1966.

4. Almy, Millie. "Spontaneous Play: An Avenue for Intellectual Development." *Bulletin of the Institute of Child Study.* 28: 2-15. 1966.

5. Anderson, C. Raymond. "Measuring Behavioral Learnings: A Study in Consumer Credit." (Report No. 67). Center for Social Organization of Schools. 1970.

6. Axline, Virginia M. "Play Therapy and Race Conflict in Young Children." *Journal of Abnormal and Social Psychology.* 43: 300-310. 1948.

7. Baker, Eugene. "A Pre-Civil War Simulation for Teaching American History" in *Simulation Games in Learning* (Boocock and Schild, Eds.). Beverly Hills: Sage Publications, Inc. 1968.

8. Bettelheim, Bruno. "Play and Education." *School Review.* 81: 1-13. November 1972.

9. Boocock, Sarane S., and James S. Coleman. "Games with Simulated Environments in Learning." *Sociology of Education.* 39: 215-236. Summer 1966.

10. Brodbelt, Samuel. "Simulation in the Social Studies: An Overview." *Social Education.* 33: 176-178. February 1969.

11. Chartier, Myron R. "Learning Effect—An Experimental Study of a Simulated Game and Instrumented Discussion." *Simulation and Games.* 3: 203-218. June 1972.

12. _____. "The Ten Commandments for Game Facilitators." *Simulation-Gaming-News.* 11: 8-9. March 1974.

13. Chapin, June R. "Simulation Games." *Social Education.* 33: 798-800. October 1969.

14. Coats, James Harold. "A Comparative Study of the Effects of Simulation and Traditional Teaching on Student Achievement, Attitude, Motivation and Interpersonal Relations in Eleventh Grade American History." Doctoral Dissertation. Auburn University. 1973.

15. Coch, L., and J. R. P. French. "Overcoming Resistance to Change." *Human Relations.* 1: 512-532. 1948.

16. Cohen, Karen C. "Effects of the Consumer Game on Learning and Attitudes of Selected Seventh Grade Students in a Target-Area School." (Report No. 65). Center for Social Organization of Schools. 1970.

17. _____. "The Effects of Two Simulation Games on the Opinions and Attitudes of Selected Sixth, Seventh, and Eighth Grade Students." (Report No. 42). Center for the Social Organization of Schools. 1969.

18. Cullen, Lieutenant Commander Charles. "From the Kriegsacademie to the Naval War College: The Military Planning Process." *Naval Review.* 22: 6-16. January 1970.

19. DeKock, Paul. "Simulations and Changes in Racial Attitudes." *Social Education.* 33: 181-183. February 1969.

20. Dempsey, Richard. "Reducing Educational Pressures." *Science.* 157: 1117-1125. 1967.

21. D'Heurle, Adma, and Joel N. Fiemer. "On Play." *The Elementary School Journal.* 72: 118-124. December 1971.

22. Edwards, Keith J. "The Effect of Ability, Achievement, and Number of Plays." (Report No. 115). Center for Social Organization of Schools. 1971.

23. Edwards, Keith. "Students' Evaluations of a Business Simulation Game as a Learning Experience." (Report No. 121). Center for Social Organization of Schools. 1971.

24. Edwards, Keith J., and David L. DeVries. "Learning Games and Student Teams: Their Effects on Student Attitudes and Achievement." (Report No. 147). Center for Social Organization of Schools. 1972.

25. Edwards, Keith J., David L. DeVries and John P. Snyder. "Games and Teams." *Simulation and Games.* 3: 247-269. September 1972.

26. Entwisle, Doris R. "Giant Steps: A Game to Enhance Semantic Development of Verbs." (Report No. 81). Center for Social Organization of Schools. 1970.

27. Farran, Dale C. "Games Work With Underachievers." *Scholastic Teacher.* 10-11. November 9, 1967.

28. Finch, Curtis R., and Patrick A. O'Reilly. "The Effects of Simulation on Problem Solving Development." *Simulation and Games.* 5: 47-71.

29. Flanders, N. A. "Personal-Social Anxiety as a Factor in Experimental Learning Situations." *Journal of Educational Research.* 45: 100-110. October 1951.

30. _____. Teacher Influence, Pupil Attitudes and Achievement: Studies in Interacter Analysis. Minneapolis: University of Minnesota. 1960.

31. Fleishman, E. A., and E. F. Harris. "Patterns of Leadership Behavior Related to Employee Grievances and Turnover." *Personnel Psychology.* 15: 43-56. 1962.

32. Flether, Jerry L. "Evaluation of Learning in Two Social Studies Simulation Games." *Simulation and Games.* 2: 259-286. September 1971.

33. Garvey, Dale M., and W. H. Seiler. A Study of Effectives of Different Methods of Teaching International Relations to High School Students. (Final Report, Cooperative Research Project No. S-270). Emporia: Kansas State Teachers College. 1966.

34. Gilliom, M. Eugene. "Trends in Simulation." *The High School Journal.* 58: 265-272. April 1974.

35. Goodman, F. L. "Simulation and Gaming" in *Handbook of Research on Teaching* (R. Travers. Ed.). Chicago: Rand McNally and Co. 1973.

36. Gordan, Alice Kaplan. *Games for Growth.* Chicago: Science Research Associates. 1970.

37. Heitzmann, Wm. Ray, and Charles E. Staropoli. "Social Science Simulations and Attitudinal Change." *South-*

western Journal of Social Education. 3: 11-14. Spring-Summer 1974.

38. Heitzmann, Wm. Ray. "The Validity of Social Science Simulations: A Review of Research Findings." *Education.* 94: 33-37. December 1973.

39. Inbar, Michael. "The Differential Impact of a Game Simulating a Community Disaster." *The American Behavioral Scientist.* 10: 18-27. October 1966.

40. Jersild, Arthur T. *Child Psychology.* Englewood Cliffs, N.J.: Prentice Hall. 1960.

41. Kidder, Steven J., and John T. Guthrie. "The Training Effects of a Behavior Modification Game." (Report No. 116). Center for Social Organization of Schools. 1971.

42. Kidder, Steven J., and Horace E. Aubertine. "Attitude Change and Number of Plays of a Social Simulation Game." (Report No. 145). Center for Social Organization of Schools. 1972.

43. Klietsch, Ron. "Involvement Learning. . .What's It All About." *ISI Product.* 4. 1972-1973.

44. Lewin, Kurt. *Dynamic Theory of Personality.* New York: McGraw-Hill. 1935.

45. Lewin, K., R. Lippitt, and R. K. White. "Patterns of Aggressive Behavior in Experimentally Created Social Climates." *Journal of Social Psychology.* 10: 271-299. 1939.

46. Lieberman, J. Nina. "Playfulness and Divergent Thinking: An Investigation of Their Relationship at the Kindergarten Level." *Journal of Genetic Psychology.* 108: 219-224. 1966.

47. Lindgren, H. C., and F. Lindgren. "Creativity Brainstorming and Orneriness as Facilitators of Creativity." *Psychological Reports.* 16: 577, 583. 1965.

48. Livingston, Samuel A. "Simulation Games and Attitudes Toward the Poor: Three Questionnaire Studies." (Report No. 118). Center for Social Organization of Schools. 1971.

49. Livingston, Samuel, and Clarice Stasz Stoll. *Simulation Games.* New York: The Free Press. 1973.

50. McFarlane, Paul T. "Pilot Studies of Role Behaviors In A Parent-Child Simulation Game." (Report No. 39). Center for Social Organization of Schools. 1969.

51. McKenney, James L. "An Evaluation of a Business Game in an MBA Curriculum." *The Journal of Business.* 35: 278-286. 1962.

52. McKenney, James L., and William R. Dill. "Influences on Learning in Simulations Games." *The American Behavioral Scientist.* 10: 28-32. October 1966.

53. McMurrin, Sterling M. *Toward Humanistic Education: A Curriculum of Affect.* Ford Foundation Report. 1970.

54. Mager, Robert F. *Developing Attitude Toward Learning.* Belmont, California: Fearon Publishers. 1968.

55. Maxon, Robert C. "Simulation: A Method That Can Make A Difference." *The High School Journal.* 57: 107-111. December 1973.

56. Michelman, Shirley. "The Importance of Creative Play." *The American Journal of Occupational Therapy.* 25: 285-290. 1971.

57. Millar, Susanna. *The Psychology of Play*. Middlesex, England: Penguin Books. 1968.

58. Neman, John Joseph. "Effectiveness of an Educational Simulation in Teaching Ethnic Studies to High School Students." Doctoral Dissertation. Northern Illinois University. 1974.

59. Nesbitt, William A. *Simulation Games for the Classroom*. New York: The Foreign Policy Association. 1971.

60. Palacino, Vincent. "A Comparable Study of the Effectiveness of Simulation in Changing Regular Teachers' Attitudes toward the Integration of Exceptional Children into the Regular Classroom." Doctoral Dissertation. Michigan State University. 1973.

61. Pfeiffer, I. L. "Teaching in Ability Grouped English Classes: A Study of Verbal Interaction and Cognitive Goals." *Journal of Experimental Education*. 36: 33-38. 1967.

62. Piaget, Jean. *Play Dreams and Imitation in Childhood*, translated by C. Gattegno and F. M. Hodgson. New York: W. W. Norton and Company, Inc. 1962.

63. Rosen, Benson, Thomas H. Jerdee, and W. Harvey Hegarty. "Effects of Participation in a Simulated Society on Attitudes of Business Students." *Journal of Applied Psychology*. 57: 335-337. 1973.

64. Ryan, T. Antoinette. "Use of Simulation To Increase Transfer." *The School Review*. 76: 246-252. June 1968.

65. Schild, E. O. "The Shaping of Strategies." *The American Behavioral Scientist.* 10: 1-4. November 1966.

66. Selvin, H. D. *The Effects of Leadership.* New York: The Free Press. 1960.

67. Shulman, Lee S., and Pinchas Tamir. "Research on Teaching in the Natural Sciences." *Handbook on Research in Teaching* (Ed., R. M. Travers). Chicago: Rand McNally. 1973.

68. Stern, G. C. "Measuring Non-Cognitive Variables in Research on Teaching." *Handbook of Research on Teaching* (Ed., N. L. Gage). Chicago: Rand McNally. 1963.

69. Sutton-Smith, Brian. "Child's Play—Serious Business." *Psychology Today.* 5: 68-69, 87. December 1971.

70. Torrence, E. P. "Influence of Dyadic Interaction on Creative Functioning." *Psychological Reports.* 26: 391-394. 1970.

71. Twelker, Paul A. "Some Reflections on Instructional Simulation and Gaming." *Simulation and Games.* 2: 145-153. June 1972.

72. Zuckerman, David W., and Robert E. Horn. *The Guide to Simulations/Games.* Lexington, Mass.: Information Resources, Inc. 1973.

GENERAL REFERENCES

Abt, Clark C. *Serious Games.* New York: Viking Press. 1970. This particular work is useful for three reasons; first it provides a good general background, theory and history of the field. Second, it provides some interesting anecdotes about some of the games developed by Abt Associates, professional game designers. Third, it gives some insight into the ideas of one of the leading professional game designers.

Anderson, C. Raymond. "Changing Behavior with Simulations." *Changing Times—Teacher's Journal.* December 1970. A very short but valuable introduction to simulations. This essay would be particularly useful to the novice.

Boocock, Sarane S., and E. O. Schild. (Eds.). *Simulation Games in Learning.* Beverly Hills: Sage Publications. 1968. A selection of essays by noted game designers and researchers dealing with theory and research. This is one of the notable books in the field for its discussion of the development, practice, and future of learning games. Appendices provide additional useful information.

Coleman, James. "Learning through Games." *NEA Journal.* 36. January 1967. A philosophical argument for the value of educational games as well as a theoretical rationale for their use.

Glazier, Ray. *How To Design Educational Games.* Cambridge: Games Central (Abt Associates). 1971. A nice "how to" manual useful to those who wish to construct their own simulations. It provides an outline of the steps and strategies involved. This small booklet is a must in designing teacher-made games.

Gordon, Alice Kaplan. *Games For Growth.* Palo Alto: Science Research Associates. 1970. A summary of the field which comments on the main components involved in learning games and discusses several of the commercial games. In addition, it contains a game, *Fixit.*

Guetzkow, Harold (Ed.). *Simulation in Social Science.* Englewood Cliffs, N.J.: Prentice-Hall, Inc. 1962. One of the early treatments of the learning value of simulations by several authors. This is an advanced treatment of the field as used in college classrooms, business, and by the military. Because of the approach and terminology, it would not be useful to novices.

Inbar, Michael, and Clarice S. Stoll. *Simulation Gaming in Social Science.* New York: The Free Press. 1971. An introduction to the field by the authors, as well as several essays by additional selected authors. In addition, procedures for designing simulations are included.

Kraft, Ivor. "Peadagogical Futility in Fun and Games." *NEA Journal.* 36. January 1967. A philosophical argument against using learning games in education. Useful if one wishes to read a minority position on the question.

Millar, Susanna. *The Psychology of Play.* Baltimore, Maryland: Penguin Books, Inc. 1968. A paperback that explores the topic of play through an historical and psychological analysis. The author in an exhaustive study makes a good case for the importance of play in development.

Nesbitt, William A. *Simulation Games for the Social Studies Classroom.* New York: Foreign Policy Association. 1971. A short explanation of the field. While examples are related to the social sciences it can be useful to teachers of other subject areas also. In addition, it contains a list of some commercially available games.

Simulation-Gaming-News. Box 3039 University Station, Moscow, Idaho 83843. This is a newspaper which treats the entire gamut of simulations and games. In quality journalistic style the paper carries news conferences, meeting reports, book reviews, reviews of simulations and games, as well as games and simulations. For those wishing to become more involved in the field it is a must to keep abreast of the developments. Published five times a year; the subscription rate is $4.00.

Simulation and Games. Sage Publications, Inc. 275 South Beverly Drive, Beverly Hills, California 90212. A scholarly journal containing articles reporting the results of experimental studies and theoretical discussions related to the development of the field.

Twelker, Paul A. *Instructional Simulation Systems.* Corvallis, Oregon: Continuing Education Publications. 1969. A selected annotated bibliography of games, papers, articles, books and technical reports in every subject area related to simulations. The book is laid out in a useful format to make location of references efficient for the user, with a subject index as well as an alphabetical listing.

Wing, Richard L. "Simulation as a Method of Instruction in Science Education." *Science Teacher.* 35: 41-42. May 1968. The author, an experienced game designer, explores the value of simulation in science teaching in a short article.

Zuckerman, David W., and Robert E. Horn. *Guide to Simulations/Games.* Lexington: Information Resources. 1973. This update of their previous work contains descriptions of over 600 games in all subject areas. In addition, the work provides information on how to use simulations in the classroom and advice on game design. It is the most comprehensive directory in the field.